Contents

IRELAND THE SONGS VOLUME 4

ISBN 1 85720 062 4

Copyright © 1993 **Walton Manufacturing Ltd.**
Unit 6a Rosemount Park Drive, Rosemount Business Park,
Ballycoolin Road, Dublin 11. Ireland.
US Distributors: The James Import Company. P.O. Box 874, New York, NY 10009, USA.

Printed in Ireland by Betaprint, Dublin

The O'Learys at the Tall Cross, Monasterboice, Co. Louth, 1925.

Dirty Old Town

The town is Salford and the song was written in 1946 by Ewan McColl
for a play called 'Landscape with Chimneys'.

I met my love by the gas - works
cry. Dreamed a dream by the old can -
al. Kissed my girl by the fact' - ry
wall. Dir- ty old town, dir- ty old town.

I heard a siren from the docks
Saw a train set the night on fire
Smelled the spring on the smoky wind
Dirty old town, dirty old town.

Clouds are drifting across the moon
Cat's are prowling on their beat
Springs a girl from the streets at night
Dirty old town, dirty old town.

I'm going to make a good sharp axe
Shining steel, tempered in the fire
I'll chop you down like an old dead tree
Dirty old town, dirty old town.

Repeat first verse

Muirsheen Durkin

"Cailíní deasa Muigheo", the lovely girls of Mayo, is the tune
to which this popular song is set.

In the days I went a courting I was
ne-ver tired re-sor-ting to the ale-house or the
play-house or ma-ny a house be-sides. I told my bro-ther
Sea-mus I'd go off and go right fa-mous, and be-
fore I'd come back a-gain I'd roam the world wide.

Chorus:
So goodbye Muirsheen Durkin I'm sick and tired of working
No more I'll dig the praties, no longer I'll be fooled
As sure as me name is Carney; I'll go off to California
Where instead of diggin' praties; I'll be diggin' lumps of gold

I've courted girls in Blarney, in Kanturk and in Killarney
In Passage and in Queenstown, that is the Cobh of Cork
So goodbye to all this pleasure for I'm going to take me leisure
And the next time you will hear from me,
Will be a letter from New York.
(CHORUS)

Goodbye to all the boys at home,
I'm sailing far across the foam
To try and make me fortune in far Amerikay;
There's gold and money plenty
For the poor and for the gentry;
And when I come back again I never more will stray.
(CHORUS)

O'Rourke, the Smithy, Rahan, Co. Offaly, 1925.

The Mermaid

The widespread popularity of this song is described by Albert Friedman
in his book 'Ballads of the English Speaking World'. There are
versions from all over England, Scotland, Canada and the U.S.
This version made popular by the Clancy Brothers
is a 19th century one from America.

Then up spoke the captain of our gallant ship
And a fine old man was he,
"This fishy mermaid has warned me of our doom,
We shall sink to the bottom of the sea."
(CHORUS)

Then up spoke the mate of our gallant ship
And a fine spoken man was he,
Sayin, "I have a wife in Brooklyn by the sea
And tonight a widow she will be."
(CHORUS)

Then up spoke the cabin-boy of our gallant ship
And a brave young lad was he,
"Oh I have a sweetheart in Salem by the sea
And tonight she'll be weeping for me."
(CHORUS)

Then up spoke the cook of our gallant ship
And a crazy old butcher was he,
"I care much more for my pots my pans
Than I do for the bottom of the sea."
(CHORUS)

Then three times 'round spun our gallant ship
And three times 'round spun she,
Three times 'round spun our gallant ship
And she sank to the bottom of the sea.
(CHORUS)

Love Thee Dearest

When one reads the words of this or any of Tom Moore's songs, it is difficult
to imagine that he was forced to challenge a man called Jeffrey to a duel
because of what he (Jeffrey) wrote about Moore in the *"Edinburgh Review"*.
"He sits down to ransack his memory for inflammatory images and
expressions and commits them laboriously to writing for the purpose of insin-
uating pollution - pollution into the minds of unknown and
unsuspecting readers." This was the general tone of the piece which must
have made the five-feet two-inch Moore bristle and todays reader,
wonder at such comments.

Love thee, dearest, love thee! No – that star is not more true
When my vows deceive thee, he will wander too.
A cloud of night, may veil his light
And death shall darken mine
But leave thee, dearest, leave thee! No – till death I'm thine!

"The Spinning Wheel",near Kenmare, 1932.

The Little Skillet Pot

This song first appeared in print in a 1947 American collection. It has the feel of an Irish song and could easily represent the fantasy of someone who had escaped the famine to America.

Did you e-ver eat col-can-non made with love-ly pick-led cream? With the flour and sca-llions blen-ded like a pic-ture in a dream? Did you e-ver make a hole on top to hold the crea-my flake, of the crea-my flav'-ry but-ter that my mo-ther used to make? Yes you did so you did so did she and so did I, and the more I think a-bout it sure the near-er I'm to cry. Oh but were-n't they the hap-py days when trou-bles we knew not? and our

mo - thers made col - can - non in the lit - tle skil - let pot.

Did you ever bring potato cake in a basket to the school,
Tucked underneath your arm with your book, your slate and rule,
And when teacher wasn't looking sure a great big bite you'd take,
Of the flowery flavoured buttered soft and sweet potato cake.
(CHORUS)

Did you ever go a-courting as the evening sun went down,
And the moon began a-peeping from behind the Hill o' Down,
As you wandered down the boreen where the leprechaun
was seen,
And you whispered loving phrases to your little fair colleen.
(CHORUS)

Bantry Fair, Co. Cork, 1930.

Croghan's Grove

The importance of a tree not just as part of the ecosystem but as a living being with a spiritual resonance for every generation is the topical subject matter of this song by Jim Kelly and published here for the first time.

This noble tree will thrive
Scaling the sky as God intended
In Croghan's glorious grove
Where battered spirits soon are mended
New lovers not yet born
Will sign this stalwart bole
Pledging with blade on bark
Eternal promise of the soul.

The Old Mill, Oughter, Co. Offaly, 1929.

The Spanish Lady

A Dublin twist to the recurring theme of the *spéirbhean* or
heavenly lady in Irish song and poetry.

As I came down through Dub-lin ci-ty at the hour of twelve at night. Who should I see but a Span-ish La-dy wash-ing her feet by can-dle light. First she washed them, then she dried them o-ver a fire of ash-y coal____ ____ In all my life I ne'er did see a maid so sweet a-bout the sole. Whack fol-the tur-ra lu-ra lad-die Whack fol-the tur-ra

lu - ra lay. Whack fol the tur - ra lu - ra lad - die whack fol the tur - ra lu - ra lay._____

As I came back through Dublin City;
At the hour of half past eight
Who should I spy but the Spanish lady;
Brushing her hair in the broad daylight
First she tossed it, then she brushed it;
On her lap was a silver comb
In all my life I ne'er did see;
A maid so fair since I did roam.
(CHORUS)

As I went back through Dublin City;
As the sun began to set
Who should I spy but the Spanish lady;
Catching a moth in a golden net
When she saw me, then she fled me,
Lifting her petticoat over her knee
In all my life I ne'er did see;
A maid so shy as the Spanish Lady.
(CHORUS)

I've wandered north and I've wandered south,
Through Stonybatter and Patrick's Close
Up and around by the Glouster Diamond;
And back by Napper Tandy's house
Old age has laid her hand on me;
Cold as a fire of ashy coals
In all my life I ne'er did see;
A maid so sweet as the Spanish Lady.
(CHORUS)

The Last Rose of Summer

"The poet of all circles", Thomas Moore wrote this song and set it to the
air "The Young Man's Dream". Moore met and befriended Robert Emmet
at Trinity College. He also wrote the song "When He Who Adores Thee"
in memory of Lord Edward Fitzgerald.

'Tis the last rose of summer left bloom - ming a -
lone. All her love - ly com - pan - ions are fa - ded and
gone. No flow'r of her kind - red No rose - bud is
ni - gh. To re- flect back her blu - shes, or to give sigh for sigh.

I'll not leave thee, thou lone one! to pine on the stem
Since the lovely are sleeping, go sleep thou with them.
Thus kindly I scatter thy leaves o'er the bed
Where thy mates of the garden lie scentless and dead.

So soon may I follow, when friendships decay
And from love's shining circle the gems drop away.
When true hearts lie wither'd and fond ones are flown
Oh! who would inhabit this bleak world alone!

Turf-cutter in the Knockmealdown Mountains, Co. Tipperary, 1929.

The Shoals of Herring

Ewan McColl, the great folk singer and song writer from the North of England wrote this song for a B.B.C. programme "Singing the Fishing". Luke Kelly made it almost a part of Irish musical tradition.

lug-ger for to hunt the bo - nny shoals of her - ring.

O the work was hard and the hours were long
And the treatment sure it took some bearing.
There was little kindness and the kicks were many
As we hunted for the shoals of herring.

O we fished the Swarth and the Broken Bank.
I was cook and I'd a quarter sharing,
And I used to sleep standing on my feet.
And I'd dream about the shoals of herring.

O we left the home grounds in the month of June,
And to canny Shiels we soon was bearing,
With a hundred cran of the silver darlings
That we'd taken from the shoals of herring.

Now you're up on deck, you're a fisherman.
You can swear and show a manly bearing
Take a turn on watch with the other fellows
While you're searching for the shoals of herring.

In the stormy seas and the living gales
Just to earn your daily bread you're daring,
From the Dover Straights to the Faroe Islands
As you're hunting for the shoals of herring.

O I earned me keep and I paid me way
And I earned the gear that I was wearing.
Sailed a million miles, caught ten-million fishes
We were sailing after shoals of herring.

conclusion: Night and day we're faring.
Come winter wave or winter gale.
Sweating or cold, growing up, growing old,
As we hunt the bonny shoals of herring.

19

I'm a Rover

From Scotland, the words of this song are very similar to those of
"The Night Visiting Song" which is closely connected with
"The Lovers Ghost" and "The Grey Cock."

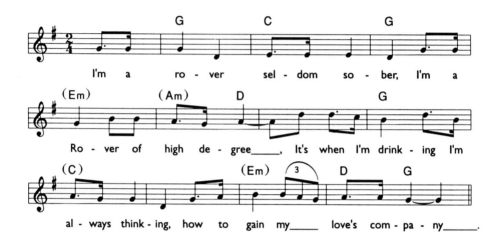

I'm a ro - ver sel - dom so - ber, I'm a
Ro - ver of high de - gree____, It's when I'm drink - ing I'm
al - ways think - ing, how to gain my____ love's com - pa - ny_____.

Though the night be as dark as dungeon
Not a star to be seen above
I will be guided without a stumble
Into the arms of my own true love.

He stepped up to her bedroom window
Kneeling gently upon a stone
He rapped at her bedroom window
'Darling dear, do you lie alone ?'

'It's only me your own true lover
Open the door and let me in
For I have come on a long journey
And I'm near drenched to the skin'.

She opened the door with the greatest pleasure
She opened the door and let him in
They both shook hands and embraced each other
Until the morning they lay as one.

The cocks were crowing, the birds were whistling
The streams they ran free about the brae,
'Remember lass, I'm a ploughman laddie,
And the farmer I must obey'.

'Now my own love, I must go and leave thee
And though the hills they are high above
I will climb them with greater pleasure,
Since I've been in the arms of my love'.

Motorised hen-coop at Carndonagh, Co. Donegal, 1929

The Banks of my own Lovely Lee

Oh how oft do my thoughts in their fan-cy take flight, to the scenes of my child-hood a - way. To the days when each pa-tri-ot's vis - ion seemed bright, ere I dreamed that those joys should de - cay. When my heart was as light as the wild winds that blow, down the Mar - dyke through each elm tree. Where I spor-ted and played 'neath each green lea-fy shade, On the banks of my own love-ly Lee. Where I spor-ted and played 'neath each green lea-fy shade, On the banks of my own love-ly Lee.

And then in the springtime of laughter and song,
Can I ever forget the sweet hours
With the friends of my youth as we rambled along
'Mongst the green mossy banks and wild flowers.
Then too, when the evening sun's sinking to rest
Sheds its golden light over the sea
The maid with her lover the wild daisies pressed
On the banks of my own lovely Lee
The maid with her lover the wild daisies pressed
On the banks of my own lovely Lee.

'Tis a beautiful land this dear isle of song
Its gems shed their light to the world.
And her faithful sons bore thro' ages of wrong
The standard St. Patrick unfurled.
Oh! would I were there with the friends I love best
And my fond bosom's partner with me
We'd roam thy banks over, and when weary we'd rest
By thy waters, my own lovely Lee.
We'd roam thy banks over, and when weary we'd rest
By thy waters, my own lovely Lee.

Oh what joys should be mine ere this life should decline
To seek shells on thy sea-gilded shore.
While the steel-feathered eagle, oft splashing the brine
Brings longing for freedom once more.
Oh all that on earth I wish for or crave
Is that my last crimson drop be for thee
To moisten the grass of my forefathers' grave
On the banks of my own lovely Lee,
To moisten the grass of my forefathers' grave
On the banks of my own lovely Lee.

Sam Hall

Credited to an Englishman, C. Ross, there are many versions of
this song from different parts of England. This one from Ireland
tells of a highwayman hanged in 1701 for robbery.

Oh they took me to Cootehill in a cart, in a cart,
Oh they took me to Cootehill in a cart,
Oh they took me to Cootehill, and 'twas there I made my will,
For the best of friends must part, so must I, so must I,
For the best of friends must part, so must I.

Up the ladder I did grope, that's no joke, that's no joke,
Up the ladder I did grope, that's no joke.
Up the ladder I did grope, and the hangman pulled his rope,
And ne'er a word I spoke, tumbling down, tumbling down,
And ne'er a word I spoke, tumbling down.

(Repeat first verse)

The stepping Stones at Ardee, Co. Louth, 1939

The Lowlands Low

This P.J. Mc Call song of south Wexford tells of the "Wild Geese", those Irish forced to flee to the continent after the Treaty of Limerick. They enlisted in the armies of those countries at war with England. The Geneva (gin) and wine on the return journey were probably smuggled goods.

Oun - more we quit - ted Mi - chael - mas gone by,
cow - hides and wool and live car - go.
Twen - ty young wild geese rea - dy fledged to fly,
sail - ing for the low - lands low. The low - lands low, the
low - lands low, sail - ing for the low - lands low.

Shaun Paor's the skipper,
From the church of Crook-
Piery keeps log for his father.
Crew all from Bannow,
Fethard and the Hook
Sailing in the Lowlands Low.

These twenty Wild Geese
Gave Queen Anne the slip,
Crossing to Lewey in Flanders.
He and Jack Malbrook
Both are in a grip,
Fighting in the Lowlands Low.

Close lay a rover
Off the Isle of Wight,
Either a Salee or Saxon.
Out through a sea mist
We bade them good night,
Sailing for the Lowlands Low.

Ready with priming
We'd our galliot gun.
Muskets and pikes in good order.
We should be riddled
Captives would be none
Death! or else the Lowlands Low.

Pray, holy Brendan,
Turk or Algerine,
Dutchman nor Saxon may sink us.
We'll bring Geneva
Rack and Rhenish wine
Safely from the Lowlands Low.

Nova Scotia

Like most sea-songs this one has been subject to much change because of
the wide-ranging nature of the sea-farers trade. This may account
for the less than traditional concept of the maid going off
to war while her man remains at home. On the other
hand it may be a very early example of role reversal.

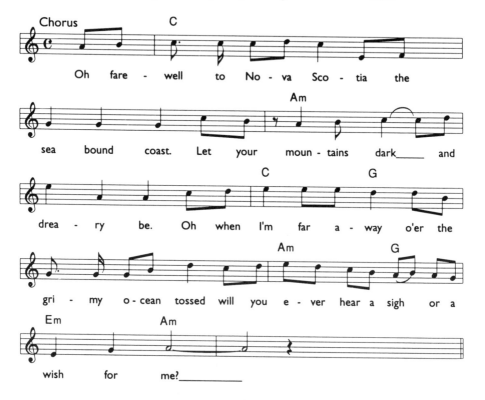

The sun it was setting in the West
And the birds were singing upon every tree
All nature seemed inclined for rest
but still there was no rest for me.
(CHORUS)

I grieve to leave my native land
And I grieve to leave my comrades all
My parents who I held so dear
And the bonny bonny lad I do adore.
(CHORUS)

Oh the drums they do beat and the wars they go on
The captain calls ye must obey
So farewell, farewell to 'Nova Scoti's' charms
For it's early in the morning and I'm far away.
(CHORUS)

Lifeboat off Inishmaan, August 1938.

29

General Munroe

In the 1798 rebellion, an Ulster Presbyterian in his early twenties led the rebel forces to victory at Saintfield. He was later defeated at Ballynahinch on June 13th and hanged three days later.

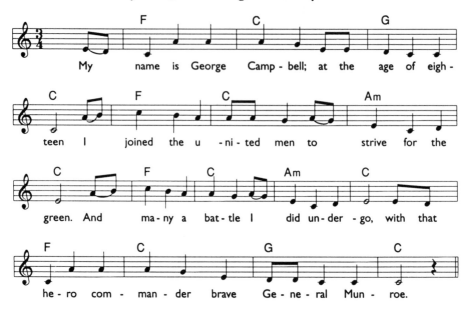

Have you heard of the Battle of Ballinahinch
Where the people oppressed rose up in defence
When Munroe left the mountains his men took the field,
And they fought for twelve hours and never did yield.

Munroe being tired and in want of a sleep,
Gave a woman ten guineas his secret to keep.
But when she got the money the devil tempted her so
That she sent for the soldiers and surrendered Munroe.

The army they came and surrounded the place,
And they took him to Lisburn and lodged him in jail.
And his father and mother in passing that way
Heard the very last words that their dear son did say !

"Oh, I die for my country as I fought for her cause,
And I don't fear your soldiers nor yet heed your laws.
And let every true man who hates Ireland's foe
Fight bravely for freedom like Henry Munroe."

And 'twas early one morning when the sun was still low,
They murdered our hero brave General Munroe,
And high o'er the Courthouse stuck his head on a spear,
For to make the United men tremble and fear.

Then up came Munroe's sister, she was all dressed in green,
With a sword by her side that was wellsharped and keen.
Giving three hearty cheers, away she did go
Saying, "I'll have revenge for my brother Munroe."

All ye good men who listen, just think of the fate
Of the brave men who died in the year Ninety Eight.
For poor old Ireland would be free long ago
If her sons were all rebels like Henry Munroe.

At Wexford Station, 1931

Flight of Earls

Written by Liam Reilly of Bagatelle, it is one of a trilogy of songs on the
theme of modern emigration.

I can hear the bells of Dublin in this lone - ly wait - ing room and the pap - er boys are sing - ing in the rain. Not too long be-fore they take us to the air - port and the noise to get on board a trans - at - lan - tic plane. We've got no - thing left to stay for, we have no more left to say and there is - n't a - ny work for us to do.

So fare-well you boys and girls a-noth-er blood-y flight of Earls. Our best as-set___ is our best ex - port too.___

It's not murder, fear or famine
that makes us leave this time.
We're not going to join McAlpines fusiliers.
We've got brains and we've got vision.
We've got education too
But we just can't throw away these precious years
So we walk the streets of London
and the streets of Baltimore
And we meet at night in several Boston bars.
We're the leaders of the future
But we're far away from home
And we dream of you beneath the Irish stars

As we look on Ellis Island and the Lady in the Bay
and Manhatten turns to face another Sunday
We just wonder what your doing
For to bring us all back home
As we look forward to another Monday.
Because it's not the work that scares us
We don't mind an honest job
And we know things will get better once again.
So a thousand times adieu
We've got Bono and U2
And all we're missing is the Guinness and the rain.

So switch off our new computers .
Cause the writing's on the wall
we're leaving as our fathers did before
Take a look at Dublin airport
or the boat that leaves Northwall
There'll be no youth unemployment anymore
Because we're over here in Queensland
And in parts of New South Wales
We're on the seas and airways and the trains
And if we see better days
Those big airplanes go both ways
And we'll all be coming home to you again.

Threshing at St. Stanislaus College, Tullabeg, Co. Offaly, 1929.

The Merry Ploughboy

A song that grew out of the 1916 Rising and became popular with the Fianna boy scouts, an important part of the Republican movement.

Oh I am a mer-cy plough-boy and I plough the fields all day. Till a sud-den thought came to my mind, that I should run a-way. Well I've al-ways hat-ed slav-er-y since the day that I was born. So I'm off to join the I. R. A. and I'm off to-mor-row morn.

Chorus

And I'm off to Dub-lin in the green in the green where the hel-mets glis-ten in the sun. Where the bay'-nets flash and the rif-fles crash to the e-cho of a Thomp-son gun.

I'll leave aside my pick and spade
And I'll leave aside my plough
I'll leave aside my old grey mare
For no more I'll need them now
And I'll leave aside my Mary,
She's the girl that I adore
Well I wonder if she'll think of me;
When she hears the cannons roar
(CHORUS)

And when this war is over
And dear old Ireland's free
I'll take her to the church to wed
And a rebel's wife she'll be.
(CHORUS)

Ploughing in the Golden Vale, Co. Tipperary, 1929.

Come Back Paddy Reilly

Percy French, that great troubadour of 19th century Ireland,
wrote this song and many more which never seem to grow stale.

Come back Pad-dy Reil - ly to Bal- ly - james - duff, come home Pad-dy Reil - ly to me._____

My mother once told me that when I was born,
The day that I first saw the light.
I looked down the street on that very first morn
And gave a great crow of delight
Now most new born babies appear in a huff
And start with a sorrowful squall
But I knew I was born in Ballyjamesduff
And that's why I smiled at them all.
That baby's a man now, he's toil worn and tough
Still whispers come over the sea.
Come back Paddy Reilly to Ballyjamesduff
Come home Paddy Reilly to me.

Joe Hill

An American song which gained great popularity with many singers and
listeners in Ireland. The music by Earl Robinson and the words by Alfred
Hayes tell the sad story of Joe Hillstrom, a young Swedish immigrant to
the US. He became an effective labour union organiser throughout
the West. He did however antagonise some very powerful people
and was convicted in very doubtful circumstances of murder
and executed in Utah in 1915 by firing squad.

I dreamed I saw Joe Hill last night a-
live as you or me, Said I, "But Joe you're
ten years dead," "I ne - ver died," said he, "I
ne - ver died," said he.

'In Salt Lake, Joe, by God' says I, him standing by my bed
They framed you on a murder charge,
Says Joe 'But I ain't dead', says Joe 'But I ain't dead',

'The copper bosses killed you Joe, They shot you Joe' says I.
'Takes more than guns to kill a man,'
says Joe, 'I didn't die' says Joe 'I didn't die'.

And standing there as big as life, and smiling with his eyes
Joe says 'What they forgot to kill
Went on to organise, went on to organise'.

'Joe Hill ain't dead' he says to me. Joe Hill ain't never died
Where workingmen are out on strike,
Joe Hill is at their side, Joe Hill is at their side.

From San Diego up to Maine, in every mine and mill
Where workers strike and organise,
Says he 'You'll find Joe Hill' says he, 'You'll find Joe Hill.'

Saving turf near Tubbercurry, Co.Sligo, 1932.

The Emigrant's Letter

In 1910 when on tour to America on board ship, Percy French over-
heard a conversation between two young men, emigrants from
Donegal. "They'll be cutting the corn in Creeshla today" was the sad
comment that inspired this song.

Dear dad-dy I'm ta-king the pen in my hand, to
tell you we're just out of sight of the land. On a grand o-cean
li-ner we're sai-ling in style, And we're sai-ling a-way from the
E-me-rald Isle. And a queer sort of hush came o-ver us
all, as the waves hid the last part of old Do-ne-gal. And it's
well to be you that is ta-king your tay, Where they're
cut-ting the corn in Creesh-la to-day.

I spoke to the captain - he won't turn her round,
And if I swum back I'd be apt to be drowned,
I'll stay where I am, for the diet is great
The best of combustibles piled on me plate.

42

But though it is 'Sumpchus', I'd swop the whole lot
For the ould wooden spoon and the stirabout pot,
And Kitty foreninst me a-wettin' the tay
Where they're cutting the corn in Creeshla today.

There's a woman on board who knows Katey by sight
So we talked of old times 'til they put out the light.
I'm to meet the good woman tomorra' on deck
And we'll talk about Katey from this to Quebec.
I know I'm no match for her - oh! not the leesht,
With her house and two cows and her brother a preesht.
But the woman declares Katey's heart's on the say
And mines back with Katey in Creeshla the day.

If Katey is courted by Patsey or Mick,
Put a word in for me with a lump of a stick,
Don't kill Patsey outright, he had no sort of chance
But Mickey's a rogue you might murther at wance.
For Katey might think as long as she waits,
A boy in the hand is worth two in the States.
And she'll promise to honour, to love and obey
Some rover that's roamin' round Creeshla the day.

Goodbye to you, Dan, there's no more to be said,
And I think the salt wather's got to my head.
For it dreeps from me eyes when I call to my mind,
The friends and the Colleen I'm leaving behind.
But still she might wait, whin I bid her goodbye,
There was just the last taste of a tear in her eye,
And a break in her voice whin she said, 'You might stay,
But plaze God you'll come back to ould Creeshla some day'.

The Foggy Dew

A priest Father O'Neill, wrote this tribute to the men who died
in the Easter rising in Dublin in 1916.

Right proudly high in Dublin Town
they flung out the flag of war
'Twas better to die 'neath an Irish sky
than at Suvla or Sud El Bar;
And from the plains of Royal Meath
strong men came hurrying through
While Britannia's huns with their great big guns,
sailed in through the Foggy Dew.

O the night fell black and the rifles' crack
made "Perfidious Abion" reel.
'Mid the leaden rail, seven tongues of flame
did shine o'er the lines of steel;
By each shining blade, a prayer was said
that to Ireland her sons be true
And when morning broke still the war flag shook
out its fold in the Foggy Dew.

'Twas England bade our Wild Geese go
that small nations might be free
But their lonely graves are by Suvla's waves
or the fringe of the Great North Sea
O had they died by Pearse's side,
or had fought with Cathal Brugha
Their names we'd keep where the Fenians sleep,
'neath the shroud of the Foggy Dew.

But the bravest fell, and the requiem bell
rang mournfully and clear
For those who died that Eastertide
in the springtime of the year
While the world did gaze, with deep amaze,
at those fearless men, but few
Who bore the fight that Freedom's light
might shine through the Foggy Dew.

Ah, back through the glen I rode again,
and my heart with grief was sore
For I parted then with valiant men
whom I never shall see more
But to and fro in my dreams I go
and I'd kneel and pray for you
For slavery fled, O glorious dead,
when you fell in the Foggy Dew.

At Limerick Docks, 1936.

Cliffs of Dooneen

An emigrant's song about the beauties and charms of Dooneen Point
which lies six miles north of Ballybunion in County Kerry.

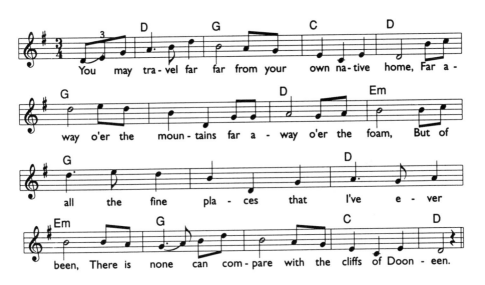

It's a nice place to be on a fine summer's day.
Watching all the wild flowers that ne'er do decay.
Oh, the hare and the pheasant are plain to be seen,
Making homes for their young 'round the Cliffs of Dooneen.

Take a view o'er the mountains fine sights you'll see there.
You'll see the high rocky mountains on the west coast of Clare,
Oh the towns of Kilkee and Kilrush can be seen,
From the high rocky slopes 'round the Cliffs of Dooneen.

So fare thee well to Dooneen fare thee well for a while
And although we are parted by the raging sea wild,
Once again I will wander with my Irish colleen, ·
'Round the high rocky slopes of the Cliffs of Dooneen.

Biddy Mulligan

I'm a fine bux-om wid-ow I live in a spot in Dub-lin they call it The Coombe.___ Me shops and me stalls are laid out in the street, and me pal-ace con-sists of one room.___ I sell app-les and or-an-ges nuts and sweet peas, ba-na-nas and su-gar stick sweet.___ On Sat-ur-day night I sell se-cond hand clothes from the floor of my stall in the street.___ You may tra-vel from Clare to the Coun-ty Kil-dare from Fran-cis Street back to the Coombe.___ But

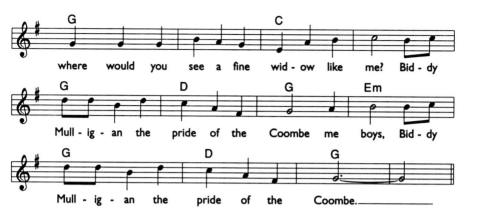

where would you see a fine wid-ow like me? Bid-dy
Mull-ig-an the pride of the Coombe me boys, Bid-dy
Mull-ig-an the pride of the Coombe.

I sell fish on a Friday spread out on a board.
The finest you'd find in the sea.
But the best is my herrings, fine Dublin Bay herrings,
There's herrings for dinner and tea.
I have a son Mick, he's great on the flute,
He plays in the Longford Street Band.
It would do your heart good to see him march out,
On a Sunday for Dollymount Strand.
(CHORUS)

In the Park on a Sunday I cut quite a dash.
The neighbours look on with surprise.
With my Aberdeen shawlie thrown over my head,
I dazzle the sight of their eyes.
At Patrick Street corner for sixty-four years,
I've stood and no one can deny.
That while I stood there, no one could dare,
To say black was the white of my eye.
(CHORUS)

Now I'm Easy

Eric Bogle who wrote this song and among others "The Band Played Waltzing Matilda" is almost unbelievably not a son of the Australian out-back. He was born in Peebles in Scotland and lived there until he was twenty-five when he took off for New South Wales.

For near - ly six - ty years I've been a
cock - y_____, Through drought fire and
flood I've lived plen - ty_____, This
coun - try's dust and mud has seen my tears and
blood. But it's near - ly o - ver now, And now I'm
ea - sy_____

I married a fine young girl when I was twenty;
But she died in giving birth when she was thirty,
No flying Doctor then,
Just a gentle old black gin;
But it's nearly over now,
And now I'm easy.

50

She left me with two sons and a daughter;
And a bone-dry farm whose soil cried out for water,
My care was rough and ready,
But they grew up fine and steady;
But it's nearly over now,
And now I'm easy.

My daughter married young, and went her own way;
My sons lie buried by the Burma Railway;
So on the land I've made my own,
I've carried on alone,
But it's nearly over now,
And now I'm easy.

City folks these days despise the cocky,
Say with subsidies and all, we've had it easy,
But there's no drought or starving stock,
On your sewered suburban block,
But it's nearly over now,
And now I'm easy.

Repeat first verse.

Bound Down for Newfoundland

Another of the sea songs which came back with the sailors.
This one is probably of English origin.

On St. Pa - trick's Day the se - ven - teenth from New York we set sail. Kind for - tune did fa - vour us with a sweet and a pleas - ant gale. We bore a - way from A - mer - i - kay the breeze be - ing off the land. And with courage brave we ploughed the wave bound down for New - found - land.

Our captain's name was Nelson, just twenty years of age.
As true as brave a sailor man as ever ploughed the wave.
The even' in our brig was called,
The longing to remain
And with courage brave we ploughed the wave
Bound down for Newfoundland.

Just three days out to our surprise, our captain he fell sick
In short he was not able to take his turn on deck.
The fever raged which made us think that death was near at hand
So we sailed away from Arasat
Bound down for Newfoundland.

All that night long we did lament, for our departed friend.
And we were praying unto God for what had been his end.
We prayed that God might guard us and keep us by his hand
And send us fair wind while at sea.
Bound down for Newfoundland.

"Old and New": bee-hive hut at Slea Head, with Blasket Islands in the distance. Co. Kerry, 1929.

Meet me at the Pillar

I was walk-ing down by Is-land Bridge, just
go-ing as I pleased.____ The same blue day the sun was warm.__
____ There was just a gent-le breeze. I
walked up by the old stone steps, in to the Phoen-ix Park.
____ Watched the child-ren run and play
____ in the hours be-fore the dark.____ I

Chorus
Meet me at the Pill-ar son. Please meet me there at noon.
____ I need you brave young I-rish-men.____

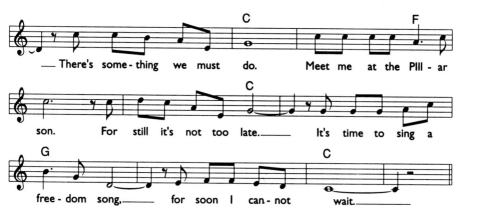

There's some-thing we must do. Meet me at the Pill-ar son. For still it's not too late.___ It's time to sing a free-dom song,___ for soon I can-not wait.___

I walked up to the monument
And lay there on the ground.
In the distance I could hear the drums.
I heard the battle sound
And I don't know what came over me
For a moment I could hear
The pleading of a soldier boy
Kept calling in my ear.
(CHORUS)

I looked around to see this man
But nobody was there
In the distance I could hear the guns
Yet stillness filled the air.
I closed my eyes and in the stream
A soldier I could see
He said his name was Padraig Pearse
And he kept calling me.
(CHORUS)

Only our Rivers run Free

A recent song written by Michael McConnell in 1973.
The theme is a recurring one-Ireland unfree.

When apples still grow in No-vem-ber,____ When
blos-soms still bloom on each tree,____ When
leaves are still green in De-cem-ber,____ It's
then that our land will be free.____ I wan-der her
hills and green val-leys,____ but still thro' my
sor-row I see,____ a land that has ne-ver known
free-dom,____ and on-ly her ri-vers run free.____

I drink to the death of her manhood
Those men who'd rather have died
Than to live in the cold chains of bondage
To bring back their rights were denied.
Oh where are you now that we need you,
What burns where the flame used to be
Are you gone like the snow of last winter,
And will only our rivers run free ?

How sweet is life, but we're crying,
How mellow, the wine, but we're dry,
How fragrant the rose, but it's dying,
How gentle the wind but it sighs.
What good is in youth when it's ageing,
What joy is in eyes that can't see,
When there's sorrow in sunshine and flowers,
And still only our rivers run free.

Canal Barge, near Tullamore, Co. Offaly, 1929.

Master McGrath

This small black and white greyhound has two monuments to his memory,
one at Bury St. Edmunds in England and the other at his birthplace in
Colligan near Dungarvan, Co. Waterford. He won the Waterloo Cup in
1868, 1869 and 1871 and but for being doped would almost certainly
have won in 1870.

Eight-een six - ty nine being the date of the
year. Those Wat - er - loo sports - men and
more did ap - pear. For to gain the great
pri - zes and bear them a - wa' nev- er count - ing on
Ire - land and Mas - ter Mc Grath.

On the twelfth of December, that day of renown,
McGrath and his keeper they left Lurgan town
A gale in the Channel it soon drove them o'er
On the thirteenth day they landed on fair England's shore.

And when they arrived there in big London town
Those great English sportsmen they all gathered round
And some of the gentlemen gave a 'Ha, ha,'
Saying 'Is that the great dog you call Master McGrath?'

And one of these gentlemen standing around
Says 'I don't care a damn for your Irish greyhound'
And another he laughed with a scornful 'Ha, ha,
We'll soon humble the pride of your Master McGrath.'

Then Lord Lurgan came forward and said 'Gentlemen
If there's any amongst you has money to spend,
For you nobles of England I don't care a straw,
Here's five thousand to one upon Master McGrath.

Then McGrath he looked up and he wagged his old tail
Informing his Lordship 'I know what you mane,
Don't fear noble Brownlow, don't fear them agra
For I'll tarnish their laurels,' says Master McGrath.

And Rose stood uncovered, the great English pride,
Her master and keeper were close by her side;
They have her away and the crowd cried 'Hurrah'
For the pride of all England and Master McGrath.

Bunclody

Formerly called Newtownbarry, Bunclody stands at the meeting of the
Clody and Slaney rivers.

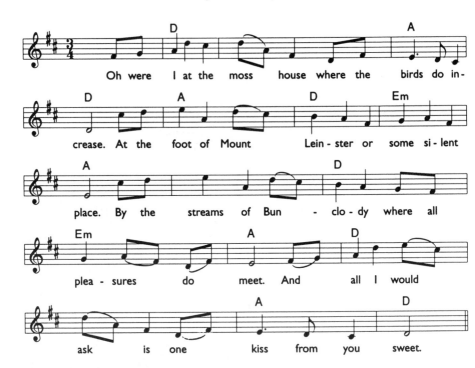

Oh were I at the moss house where the birds do in-
crease. At the foot of Mount Lein-ster or some si-lent
place. By the streams of Bun - clo-dy where all
plea-sures do meet. And all I would
ask is one kiss from you sweet.

Oh, 'tis why my love slights me as you might understand.
For she has a freehold and I have no land.
She has fine stores of riches, of silver and gold,
And everything fitting a house to uphold.

Oh were I a clerk and could write a fine hand
I would write my love a letter, that she might understand.
For I am a young fellow that was wounded in love.
Once I lived in Bunclody but now I must remove.

So fare thee well, father - my mother, adieu.
My sisters and brothers, farewell unto you.
I am bound for Amerikay, my fortune to try,
When I think of Bunclody, I am ready to die.

"A Knight of the Road", J. McGuire with his daughter Elizabeth, Roscrea, 1929.

The Star of the County Down

Cathal MacGarvey wrote this song to the air of "My Love Nell".

Near Ban - bridge town in the Coun - ty Down one mor - ning in Ju - ly, Down a bo - reen green came a sweet col - leen and she smiled as she passed me by. She looked so sweet from her two bare feet to the sheen of her nut brown hair. Such a coax - ing elf that I shook my - self to make sure she was rea - lly there. From Ban - try Bay up to Der - ry Quay and from Gal - way to Dub - lin town no

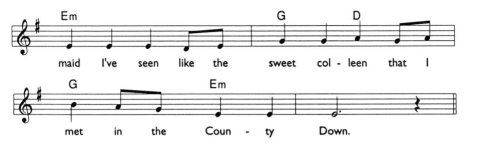

maid I've seen like the sweet col-leen that I met in the Coun-ty Down.

As she onward sped I shook my head
And I gazed with a feeling quare,
'And I said', says I to a passer by
'Who's the maid with the nut-brown hair?'
He smiled at me and with pride says he
'That's the gem of Ireland's crown.
She's young Rosie McCann from the banks of the Bann,
She's the Star of the County Down'.
(CHORUS)

She'd a soft brown eye and a look so sly
And a smile like the rose in June
And you hung on each note from her lily-white throat
As she lilted and Irish tune.
At the pattern dance you were held in a trance
As she tripped through a jig or a reel
And when her eyes she'd roll, she'd coax, upon my soul,
a spud from a hungry pie.
(CHORUS)

I've travelled a bit but never was hit,
Since my roving career began.
But fair and square I surrendered thee
To the charm of young Rosie McCann.
With a heart to let and no tenant yet,
Did I meet within a shawl or a gown
But in she went and I asked no rent
From the Star of the County Down.
(CHORUS)

At the crossroads fair I'll be surely there
And I'll dress in my Sunday clothes.
And I'll try sheep's eyes and deludhering lies
On the heart of the nut-brown Rose.
No pipe I'll smoke, no horse I'll yoke
Though my plough with rust turns brown.
Till a smiling bride by my own fireside
Sits the Star of the County Down.
(CHORUS)